7/03

TUMBLEWEEDS

#3

Tom K. Ryan

FAWCETT GOLD MEDAL • NEW YORK

TUMBLEWEEDS #3

Copyright © 1967, 1968 by The Register and Tribune Syndicate

© 1970 CBS Publications, The Consumer Publishing
Division of CBS Inc.

ISBN: 0-449-13672-8

Printed in the United States of America

13   12   11   10   9   8   7   6   5   4

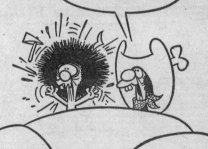

HI THERE!

GEE! DID I SCARE YA?

NOW WHAT EVER GAVE YOU THAT IDEA?

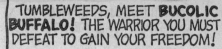

TUMBLEWEEDS, MEET **BUCOLIC BUFFALO!** THE WARRIOR YOU MUST DEFEAT TO GAIN YOUR FREEDOM!

ISN'T HE GORGEOUS? 450 POUNDS OF MUSCLE AND BONE!...

WE FEED HIM WELL, BLESS HIS HEART!

WHERE DO YOU GET THE BANANAS?

I'LL NEVER GET TO MARRY MY LITTLE PIGEON AS LONG AS HER FATHER HATES ME!... I MUST SOFTEN HIM UP!... **I'VE GOT IT!**... I'LL USE THE OLD SURE-FIRE, NEVER-FAIL, FUTURE-FATHER-IN-LAW APPROACH!...

HELLO, LITTLE PIGEON! **HI, DAD!**

WELL...BACK TO THE OL' FIASCO HATCHERY

LISTEN, YOU HAGGARD BAG OF CONCENTRATED SAG! WHEN YOUR MASTER CALLS, YOU COME!

THIS MONTH THE COVETED BLACK FEATHER GOES TO THAT BREECH-CLOTHED BEAU BRUMMEL, THAT PINK-PLUMED POPINJAY, THE BEST DRESSED BRAVE IN THE TRIBE: **ETHEREAL EAGLE**, I NAME YOU **INDIAN OF THE MONTH!**

MERCY ME! DIDN'T YOU KNOW BLACK IS DEFINITELY OUT THIS SEASON? HEAVENS TO BON TON, YOU DROLL THING! I CAN'T POSSIBLY BE SEEN IN BLACK! HOW CRASS CAN ONE GET!

TRY ME AGAIN NEXT SEASON, FELLA!

LET'S GET WITH IT, YOU SILLY SAVAGE!

OH SHUT-UP!

ISN'T IT GREAT?! IT'S **SNEAKY WEEK** AGAIN! GOOD OL' SNEAKY WEEK!..

MEDICINE MAN

THAT FAMILIAR PHENOMENON WHEN US FRUSTRATED FLAKE-OFFS FORSAKE OUR FUMBLE-FOOTED PHOBIAS AND FEEBLER FACULTIES FOR THE FACILE FAKERY 'N' FLAMBOYANT FLAIR OF FLEET-FEETED PHANTOMS O' FOLIAGE 'N' FOOTPATH! YES, **SNEAKY WEEK:** "WHEN THE URGE TO SNEAK DOTH SIEZE, ALL GOOD ABORIGINES!"

DON'T YOU AGREE?

WOULD YOU REPEAT THE QUESTION?

MEDICINE MAN

THIS MONTH, THE COVETED BLACK FEATHER GOES TO AN OLD FRIEND! THAT CONJURING CORN BALL, THAT M.D. IN MOCCASINS: **MEDICINE MAN,** I NAME YOU **INDIAN OF THE MONTH!**

ME?! GOSH! I'M OVERWHELMED! I CAN'T BELIEVE IT! WHAT A SURPRISE! TELL ME! HOW DID YOU HAPPEN TO CHOOSE ME?

OH, WE WERE SITTIN' AROUND, SCRAPING THE BOTTOM O' THE BARREL..

JUDGE, BEFORE I GO TO RESCUE KNUCKLES FROM THE INDIANS, I WANNA MAKE OUT MY LAST WILL AN' TESTAMENT...

ALL MY WORLDLY POSSESSIONS ARE IN THIS BAG: A DOLLAR AN' THIRTY-TWO CENTS, A OLD WATCH, A POLISHED STONE, A POCKET KNIFE, AN' SIX HORSESHOE NAILS! IF I DON'T RETURN, GIVE THIS TO THE MOST DESERVING PERSON IN GRIMY GULCH!

DONE, MY BOY! AND SHOULD YOU FAIL TO RETURN, MAY I TAKE THIS OCCASION TO EXTEND MY HUMBLE GRATITUDE!

CITIZENS OF GRIMY GULCH! LET'S GIVE TUMBLEWEEDS A ROUSING SEND-OFF ON HIS MISSION TO RESCUE DEAR KNUCKLES FROM THE INDIANS!

GODSPEED, LAD! AND REMEMBER! SHOULD THOSE TREACHEROUS, RED RASCALS GIVE YOU ANY TROUBLE, YOU ALWAYS KNOW WHERE YOU CAN TURN FOR HELP!...

NAUSEA JUNCTION'S RIGHT DOWN THE ROAD!

LISTEN, SHRIMP! LITTLE PIGEON IS **MY** GIRL! AN' IF YOU DON'T STAY AWAY FROM HER, I'LL BREAK EVERY BONE IN YOUR EMACIATED BODY!

IS THAT SO!

NOTHING LIKE A SNAPPY COMEBACK TO GET A FELLA OUT OF A HAIRY SITUATION!

HELP! WE'VE BEEN ROBBED!! HE ALMOST CLEANED US OUT!

DEPUTY! SNAKE-EYE JUST BROKE JAIL, TOOK MY PANTS, LOCKED ME IN THIS CELL, STOLE MY HORSE AN' ESCAPED! HE JUST LEFT, HEADING WEST!..

GET GOIN', BOY! HURRY!

YOU CAN DEPEND ON ME, CHIEF!

1-24

WHAT SIZE WAIST DO YOU TAKE?

I AM ASSUMING A NEW TITLE TO GO WITH THE NEW JUG HANDLE...

GRIMY GULCH INSTITUTE OF CRIMINAL DETENTION AND REHABILITATION

HENCEFORTH, I'LL BE KNOWN AS "THE DIRECTOR OF THE GRIMY GULCH INSTITUTE OF CRIMINAL DETENTION AND REHABILITATION"!

VERY IMPRESSIVE!

INSTITUTE OF CRIMINAL DETENTION AND REHABILITATION

AND VERY PRACTICAL!...WHEN I PULL A RAID, INSTEAD OF "CHEEZ IT! THE COPS!" THE CULPRITS MUST SHOUT "CHEEZ IT! THE DIRECTOR OF THE GRIMY GULCH INSTITUTE OF CRIMINAL DETENTION AND REHABILITATION!" AND BY THAT TIME IT'LL BE TOO LATE!

"HANDY HINTS FOR HUSBAND HUNTERS #27: APPROACH THE MALE VICTIM, NONCHALANTLY, UNTIL CLOSE ENOUGH TO GET IN A RABBIT PUNCH OR A COUPLE CHOPS TO THE KIDNEY. FOR REMEMBER, A DISABLED MALE IS A VULNERABLE MALE!"

I GET THE FEELING I SHOULD REQUEST A BLINDFOLD AND A LAST CIGARETTE

"HANDY HINTS FOR HUSBAND HUNTERS #47: REMEMBER, FUTURE BRIDE, 'HOPE SPRINGS ETERNAL'! AND SPEAKING OF 'HOPE', IS YOUR HOPE CHEST WELL STOCKED? LET'S HOPE SO (HA! HA!). WHY NOT HOP INTO TOWN RIGHT NOW, AND PICK UP SOMETHING FOR YOUR HOPE CHEST!"

TUMBLEWEEDS, IF YOU CAN WHIP OUR STRONGEST WARRIOR, I'LL SET YOU AND YOUR FRIEND FREE!...AND **NOW!** ALLOW ME TO PRESENT YOUR ADVERSARY!: **OUR PRIDE AN' JOY!**

THAT MONARCH OF MAYHEM! THAT MASTER MAULER!

....THE ONE AND ONLY **BUCOLIC BUFFALO!**

I PLEDGE ALLEGIANCE TO THE FLAG OF THE UNITED STATES OF AMERICA! AN' TO...

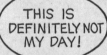

THIS MONTH, I TAKE PLEASURE IN PRESENTING THE COVETED BLACK FEATHER TO THE FIERCEST, MEANEST, NASTIEST WARRIOR IN THE TRIBE! THAT ANGRY YOUNG MAN: **TRUCULENT TOAD,** I NAME YOU **INDIAN OF THE MONTH!**

CONGRATULATIONS, MY BOY, I...

AAH SHUT-UP AN' GIMME THE STINKIN' FEATHER, MEALY MOUTH!

ARE YOU GONNA LET HIM TREAT YOUR CHIEF LIKE THAT?!

LIKE WHAT?